Contents

What is energy?

Energy makes things happen. Animals and plants can live, grow and move, and **machines** are able to **work** hard because of energy.

Electricity gives the dishwasher the energy it needs to work.

The Sun is a giant ball of burning gas that gives Earth heat and light. Energy on our planet Earth starts with the Sun.

Heat, light, sound, movement and **electricity** are all different kinds of energy.

When you run out of energy you start to feel hungry and tired, and you need to have something to eat.

We get our energy from the food we eat. This energy is stored in our muscles and we use it whenever we move.

plants

Plants don't have to hunt for food. They use energy from sunlight to make their own food from air, water and goodness in the soil.

An apple tree stores energy from sunlight in its apples. The seeds inside an apple use this energy to grow into a new apple tree.

Fruit is full of the good things a new plant needs to grow. This is why fruit is good food for you to eat.

Plants trap energy from the sun in the green colour in their leaves. They use it to make their food.

When you eat a juicy apple, you become full of energy from sunlight too.

Full of energy

You use energy day and night. How much energy you use depends on how hard you work and how busy you are.

You use up a lot of energy running and jumping because your body is working hard.

The muscles you use for moving around have a rest while you sleep.

You use less energy when you are asleep, but your body is still working. You keep breathing, your heart goes on beating and your brain keeps on working.

In your sleep, your heart beats less often and your breathing slows down.

Food

All living things and many machines need to burn **fuel** to give them energy. The fuel our bodies burn is called food.

We need to eat regular meals to keep our bodies supplied with fuel.

Food gives us energy and it helps to keep us strong and healthy too. It is important to choose food that is good for us.

Eating too much of the wrong kind of food is not good for us. Without enough food to eat, we soon become hungry, tired and weak.

You need to drink plenty of water, as well as eat food for energy.

Animals

Lions are meat-eaters. They use up a lot of energy hunting for their food. The meat they eat gives them so much energy they don't need to hunt every day.

After a good meal, lions rest and sleep. This helps them to save energy.

Some birds save energy
by **gliding** for long distances
without flapping their wings.

Birds that eat grubs and
insects work hard to find enough
food to give them energy
to fly.

Birds use up an enormous amount
of energy when they fly.

Movement and sound

There are different kinds of energy. When something moves it has movement energy.

A bus has movement energy as it drives along the road. You have movement energy too when you run to catch a bus.

This baby moves when she bangs the drum. This movement energy turns into sound energy and she hears a banging noise.

When you bang a drum you make sound energy. When you bang harder you use more energy and make a louder sound.

Heat and light

When you run around your body makes heat energy. You start to feel hot and sweaty. The faster and harder you run, the hotter and sweatier you feel.

When you sweat, little drops of water form on your skin. They help to cool you down.

Never touch a glowing
light bulb. It gives out enough heat
energy to burn you.

We use heat energy
to keep warm and
cook our food.

A light bulb gives out light and heat
energy. The thin wire inside the bulb
gets very hot and glows strongly
enough to light up a room.

Coal

Coal is a kind of fuel formed from plants that died millions of years ago. A piece of coal is full of energy.

Coal gives out heat and light energy when it burns.

The coal is brought up to the surface.
Coal is burned to give out heat energy.

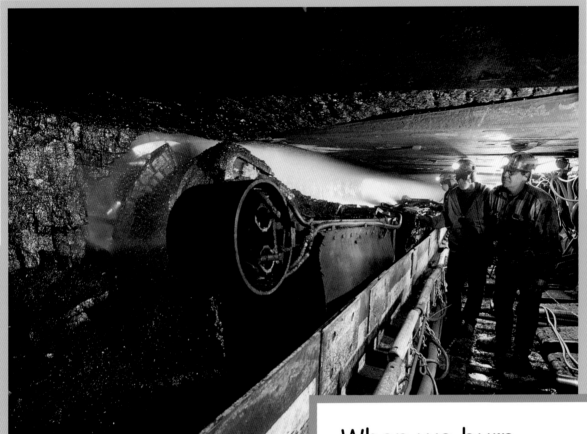

Coal is found deep underground, buried under layers of rock and soil. Miners dig out the coal with drills and big cutting machines.

When we burn coal, we are using energy from sunlight. This energy is stored in plants from millions of years ago.

Gas and oil

Gas and **oil** are two more kinds of fuel that we burn for energy. They are found deep under the ground, both on land and at the bottom of the sea.

Long pipes carry oil and gas back to land, from the oil platform out at sea.

When a car has burnt up all its petrol it runs out of energy. We have to fill it up again to keep it moving.

We cook food using the heat energy from burning gas.

Oil is made into a fuel called **petrol** in an oil refinery. A car engine burns petrol to give it the energy to move.

Electricity

Electricity is another form of energy. **Lightning** is a very powerful kind of natural electricity. We can make electricity and use it to power the things we use every day.

Coal, oil and gas are burned in power stations. This makes heat which is turned into electricity.

Electricity from power stations flows along thick **cables** to supply towns and cities.

When you turn on a switch, electricity flows along the wire and gives the television the energy it needs to work.

Electricity comes into our homes through **sockets** in the walls. Lights, heaters and machines that use electricity have plugs that are fitted into the sockets.

Batteries

A **battery** is a packet of **stored** energy. There are **chemicals** inside it. When a wire is connected to both ends of the battery, the chemicals start to change and make electricity.

A battery gives a personal stereo the energy it needs to work.

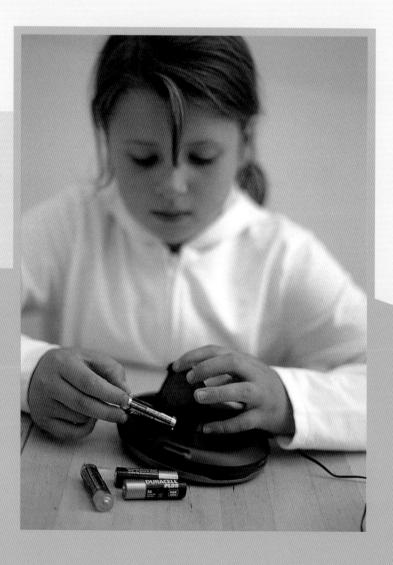

Batteries are very useful for powering small things that you need to carry around with you, such as a torch.

Machines that use batteries don't need to be plugged in to sockets.

When the chemicals inside a battery run out, they won't make any more electricity. You will need a new battery.

Sun, water and wind

We use so much energy to power machines that, one day, we will burn up all the coal, oil, and gas on Earth.

Solar panels trap energy from the sun to heat up water and make electricity.

Energy from moving water is used to make electricity in a **hydro-electric power** station.

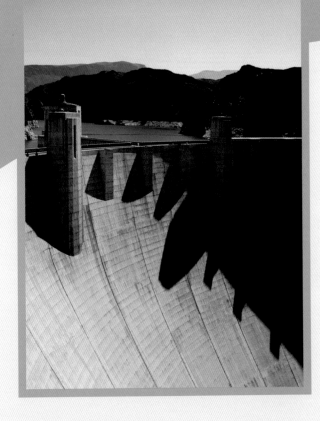

Energy from turning windmills is used to make electricity on a wind farm.

Sun, wind and water can give us energy that will never run out.

MAKE BUTTERFLIES FLUTTER

Create static electricity and watch it make tissue paper butterflies move.

YOU WILL NEED:

- coloured tissue paper
- paints
- paintbrush
- sheet of white paper
- scissors
- ping-pong ball
- length of cotton
- sticky tape

1 Cut out about six small butterfly shapes from coloured tissue paper. (About 5cm across and 3cm high.)

2 Paint three big colourful flowers on the white paper.

3 Tape the length of cotton onto the ping-pong ball.

4 Put two butterflies on each painted flower.

5 Rub the ping-pong ball against a woolly jumper for a few moments to make a kind of electricity called static electricity.

See if you can make the butterflies flutter from flower to flower.

6 Swing the ball over the butterflies. Watch the static electricity from the ball make them flutter.

Words to remember

battery A packet of stored energy used to power machines. Electricity is made when chemicals inside the battery change.

cables Long metal wires, wrapped in plastic, which carry electricity from power stations into our homes. Electricity can flow along the metal, but it cannot flow through plastic.

chemicals What everything is made up of, including our own bodies. The chemicals inside a battery make electricity.

coal A kind of fuel that gives out heat and light energy when it burns. Coal is made from plants that died millions of years ago.

electricity A kind of energy. We use electricity to power machines and other things.

energy What gives people and machines the power they need to move and work.

fuel Something that burns and makes energy that we can use to work machines or power cars. Coal, gas and oil are all kinds of fuel.

gas All around us but we can't see it. We use gas for fuel.

gliding Flying without using power. Birds glide through the air without flapping their wings. The air helps birds to float for a short time.

hydro-electric power Electricity made using the energy of fast-flowing water. A hydro-electric power station makes electricity without burning fuel.

lightning Natural electricity made in clouds during a thunderstorm. Lightning appears as a flash of light in the sky.

machine Something we use that helps to make work easier.

oil A thick black liquid found underground. It is burned as a fuel, turned into petrol and used to make materials such as plastic.

petrol Fuel made from oil. We put petrol in our cars to give them the power they need to move.

socket Where electricity comes into your home. You fit a plug into the socket to provide machines with electricity.

store To keep something to use later. You store food in a cupboard. A battery stores electricity. A piece of coal stores energy.

work What is done every time something moves, stops, gives out light or heat or makes a noise. People and machines both work.

Index